An Alphabet of Australian Birds

written by Christine Cameron

illustrated by Fiona Sinclair

Published by:
Boolarong Press,
38/1631 Wynnum Road
Tingalpa Qld 4173
Australia.
www.boolarongpress.com.au

First published 2018

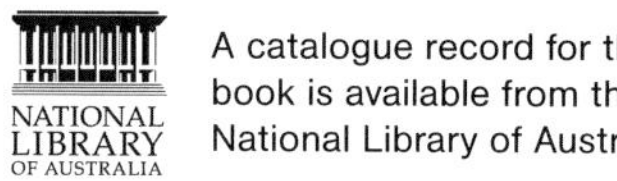

A catalogue record for this book is available from the National Library of Australia

ISBN: 9781925522983 (Paperback)

Printed and bound by Watson Ferguson & Company, Tingalpa, Australia

Dedication

To all children everywhere, keep being amazed and inspired by the beauty of birds.

Azure Kingfisher

A a

A is for Azure Kingfisher. Azure Kingfishers live along waterways where they dig burrows in the banks of rivers and streams. They love eating fish and they catch them by diving head first into the water.

Black Swan

B b

B is for Black Swan. Black Swans live on swamps and lakes. Their long necks help them reach food at the bottom of the lake. Black Swans build nests made of reeds and other wetland plants.

Crimson Rosella

C c

C is for Crimson Rosella. Crimson Rosellas live in forests and woodlands. They nest in the hollows of gum trees. They eat eucalypt seeds by holding the gum nuts in their feet while picking out the seed with their hooked beak.

Diamond Dove

Dd

D is for Diamond Dove. Diamond Doves have brilliant white spots on their wings. They make quiet cooing calls as they waddle through grasslands looking for seeds to eat. Diamond Doves make nests of grass or twigs in low shrubs or small trees.

Eastern Yellow Robin

Ee

E is for Eastern Yellow Robin. Eastern Yellow Robins have a piping call. They hunt by pouncing on insects. Eastern Yellow Robins live in forests and gardens. They build cup-like nests from bark, spider webs, and grass.

Fairy Penguin

F f

F is for Fairy Penguin. Fairy Penguins swim through the sea and they eat small fish. After feeding, they swim to the beach and waddle up to their snug burrows in the sand dunes.

Green Catbird

Gg

G is for Green Catbird. Green Catbirds live in lush rainforests and nearby gardens. Green Catbirds like to eat figs, flowers and small lizards. They build large, cup-like nests in the safety of a prickly bush or high up in a tree.

Hooded Robin

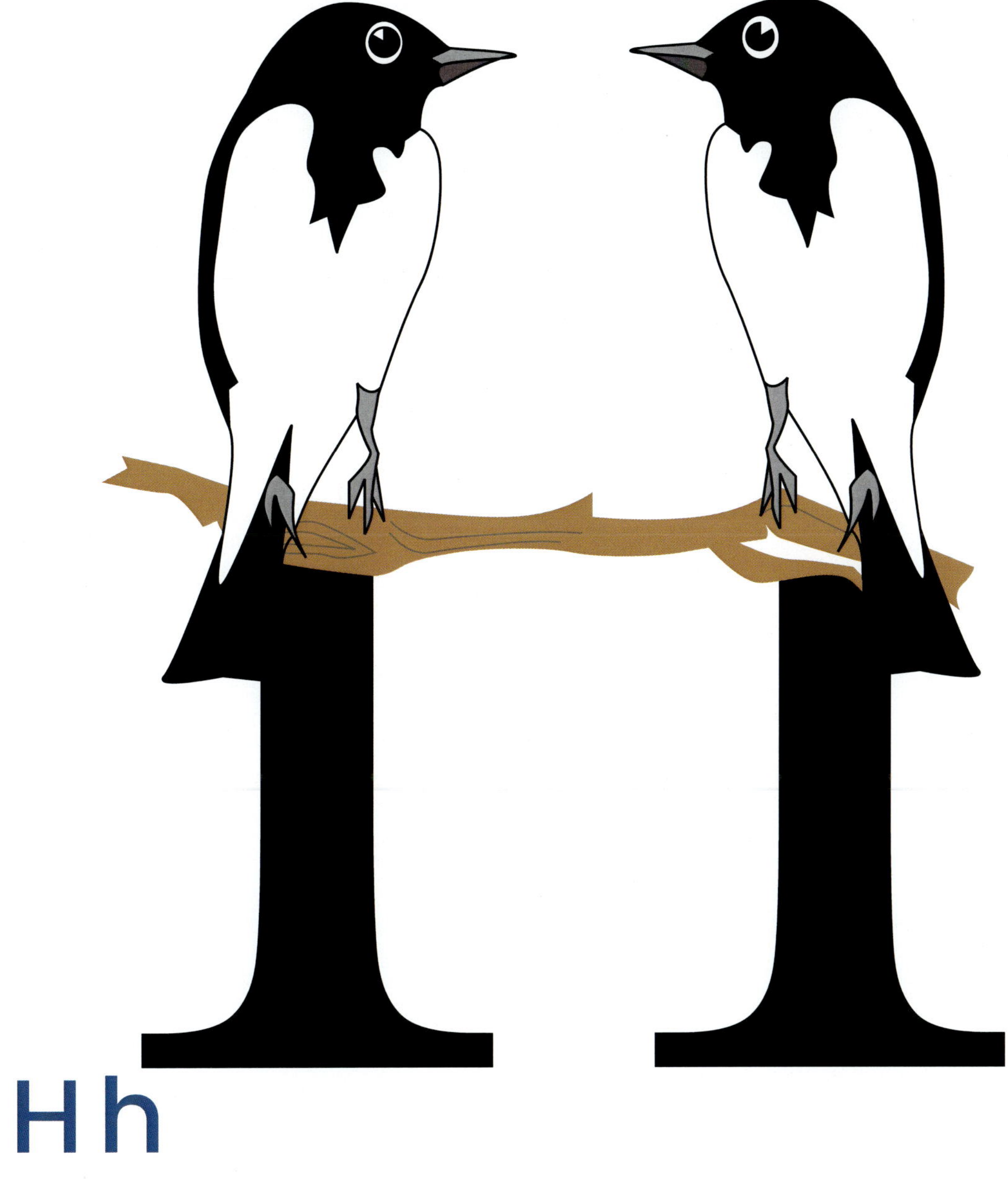

H h

H is for Hooded Robin. Hooded Robins live in dry forests and woodlands that have lots of timber on the ground. Sitting quietly on logs, they look for insects on the ground to eat. Hooded Robins build soft nests by sticking together leaves and bark with spider web, low down in a shrub or tree.

Island Thrush

I i

I is for Island Thrush. Island Thrushes live in rainforests and gardens. They catch beetles, spiders, snails and worms. Island Thrushes build cup-shaped nests high in trees. They live on Christmas Island near Australia.

Jabiru

J j

J is for Jabiru. Jabirus have long black necks. They forage for fish, eels and water pythons in rivers and swamps. Jabirus have to keep an eye out for hungry crocodiles. They build large nests of sticks up in trees.

King Parrot

Kk

K is for King Parrot. King Parrots live in forests and gardens. They are very noisy. King Parrots eat seeds, fruits, flowers and insects. They nest in deep hollows in the trunks of large, old trees.

Laughing Kookaburra

Ll

L is for Laughing Kookaburra. Laughing Kookaburras live in forests and woodlands. They are often seen in parks and gardens where you can hear their loud, cackling calls. Laughing Kookaburras nest in tree hollows, holes in riverbanks and termite mounds. Their favourite foods are small lizards and snakes.

Magpie Goose

Mm

M is for Magpie Goose. Magpie Geese dig up roots and tubers with their sharp hooked bill. They also eat grass seed. Magpie Geese live on wetlands and floodplains in large, noisy flocks. Their nests float on the water and are made by trampling water plants.

Noisy Pitta

Nn

N is for Noisy Pitta. Noisy Pittas live in rainforests where they like to eat snails, spiders and worms. They build nests of sticks and leaves. Each nest has a little opening to go in and out of and is soft and warm inside.

Orange-bellied Parrot

O o

O is for Orange-bellied Parrot. Orange-bellied Parrots are very rare. They spend summer in Tasmania where they nest in hollows in old eucalypt trees. In winter, they fly across the sea to Victoria where they feed in salt marshes.

Pink Galah

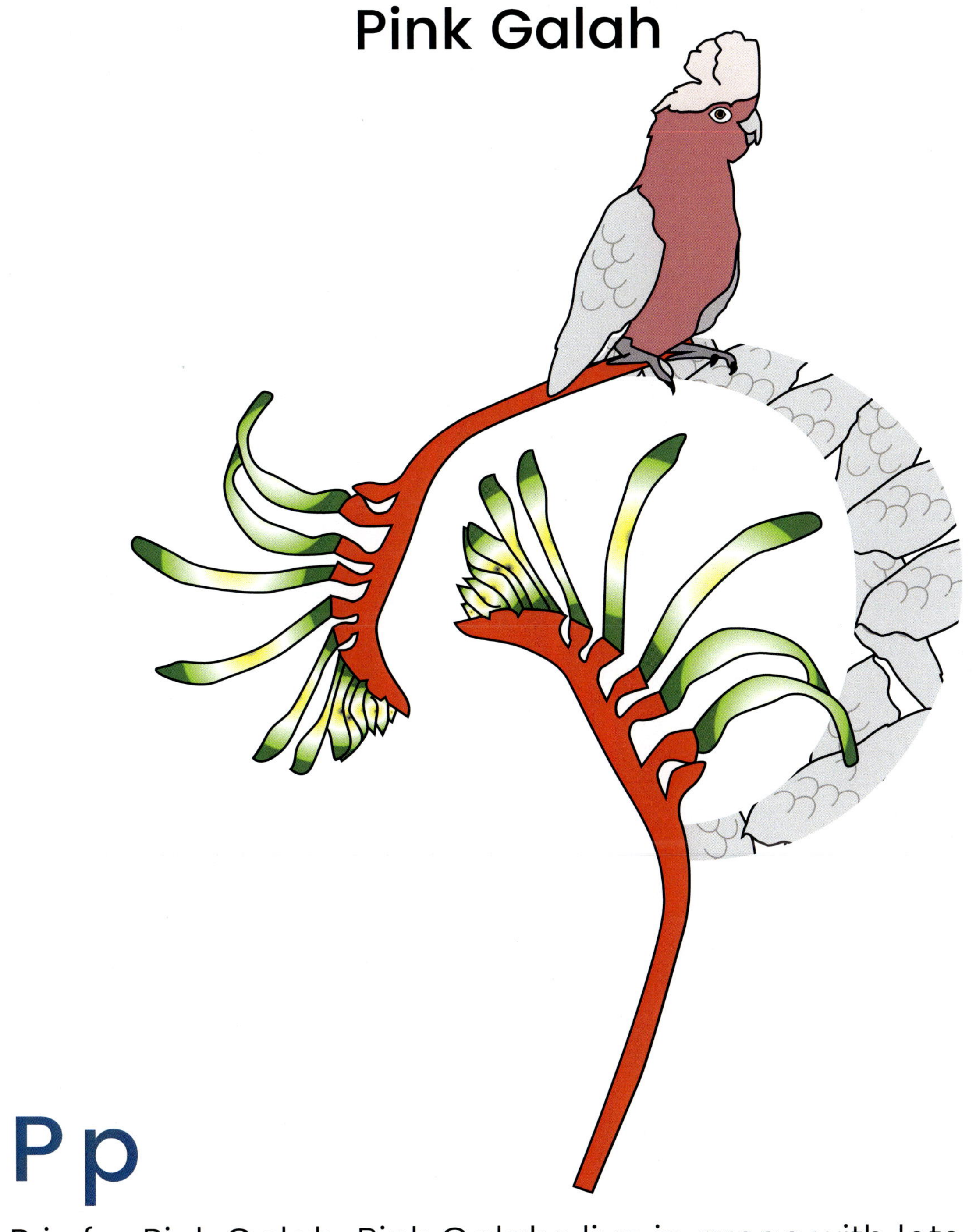

P p

P is for Pink Galah. Pink Galahs live in areas with lots of open space. You can see them in the country and the city. They eat grass seed, wattle seed, grain crops and weeds. They lay several white eggs at the bottom of tree hollows on beds of leaves.

Quail-thrush

Q q

Q is for Quail-thrush. Quail-thrush live in forests and woodlands. They move quietly along the ground looking for beetles, caterpillars, ants, and seeds to eat. They build cup-shaped nests of grass and bark on the ground next to a rock or log for shelter.

Red-tailed Black-cockatoo

R r

R is for Red-tailed Black-cockatoo. Red-tailed Black-cockatoos live in eucalypt woodlands and forests where they nest in the hollows of big, old trees. They use their large bills to chew open gum nuts to eat the seed hidden inside.

Sulphur-crested Cockatoo

S s

S is for Sulphur-crested Cockatoos. Sulphur- crested Cockatoos live in forests, parks and farmlands. They have loud screeching calls and the yellow crest on their heads stand straight up when they are excited. These noisy cockatoos will eat almost anything and they make their nests in large tree hollows.

Tree Martin

T t

T is for Tree Martin. Tree Martins live in grasslands and shrublands near rivers and lakes. They build their nests of grass and leaves in tree spouts. They catch insects to eat while flying through the air.

Upland Sandpiper

U u

U is for Upland Sandpiper. Upland Sandpipers live in grasslands. They eat beetles, grasshoppers, and crickets. Their nest is a scrape in the ground, sometimes lined with leaves and twigs. This bird has only been spotted once in Australia.

Variegated Fairy-wren

V v

V is for Variegated Fairy-wren. Variegated Fairy-wrens are shy little birds that like to stay near shrubs and bushes where they find insects and seeds to eat. They build round nests out of soft grass and spider webs, with an opening at the top to fly in and out of.

White-plumed Honeyeater

W w

W is for White-plumed Honeyeater. White-plumed Honeyeaters live in bushland as well as parks and gardens. These busy honeyeaters eat insects and also like to sip nectar from flowers. They build cosy, cup-shaped nests in the crown of a tree.

Xanthotis

X x

X is for Xanthotis macleayanus (MacLeay's Honeyeater). These honeyeaters live in rainforests and woodlands. They pick insects and spiders from the leaves and branches of trees and also like to eat fruit and nectar. They make their nests by weaving grass and feathers together and hanging them from a small branch high above the ground.

Yellow-billed Spoonbill

Y y

Y is for Yellow–billed Spoonbill. Yellow–billed Spoonbills live in swamps, shallow lakes, and farm dams. As they wade through the water, they sweep their long bills from side to side until they find a crab, yabbie or water beetle to eat. Their nests are a platform of sticks built in a tree or shrub, surrounded by water.

Zebra Finch

Z is for Zebra Finch. Zebra Finches have tail feathers that are striped like a zebra. They eat grass seeds they find in woodlands, grasslands and farmlands. Large flocks drink at waterholes and farm dams. Their nests are round with a spout on one side. They like to build their nests close together in the same shrub.

Activities

Here are some ways to learn more about birds and how to attract birds to your garden.

1. Build your own bird nest with feathers, twigs, cotton wool, playdough, clay. Make some bird eggs too.

2. Place a bird bath in your garden for birds to use. It can be made from a large pot plant saucer.

3. Count the number of birds in your garden. Use an Australian bird guide to identify them.

4. Look for bird nests in your garden.

5. Plant bird attracting plants and trees in your garden.

6. Draw a picture of your favourite bird.

OR

A Writing page:

Set out each letter with space beside it for children to trace and write each letter.

Can you remember the birds' names?

About the Author

Author, Christine Cameron: At a young age, Christine joined the Gould League of Bird Lovers. Being married to a biologist who loves birds, has meant that she is more aware of the beauty of Australian birds. From her experience as a preschool teacher, she knows that children are very interested in birds that visit their homes and educational centres. She hopes that young children will learn about the alphabet and continue to have an ongoing enjoyment and interest in all Australian birds in their lives.

Illustrator, Fiona Sinclair works with a range of imagery, but her greatest love is working with type and birds. She is a design teacher and the Education Officer and Resource coordinator for Visual Communication Victoria, preparing resources for busy design teachers to use in the secondary school classroom. Her illustrations aim to highlight the special beauty of Australian birds.